1969

STRATAGEMS TO UNCOVER NAKEDNESS

This book may be

STRATAGEMS TO UNCOVER NAKEDNESS

The Dramas of Harold Pinter

by

LOIS G. GORDON

Missouri Literary Frontiers Series Number 6

UNIVERSITY OF MISSOURI PRESS

COLUMBIA • MISSOURI

Standard Book Number 8262–8116–8
Library of Congress Card Number 68–65755
Printed in the United States of America

to Alan, with love

> The rooms we live in . . . open and shut. Can't you
> see? They change shape at their own will. I wouldn't
> grumble if only they'd keep to some consistency. But they
> don't. And I can't tell the limits, the boundaries, which
> I've been led to believe are natural.
>
> — *The Dwarfs*

The Pinter idiom is familiar but puzzling. From the one-act
The Room (1957) to the full-length *The Homecoming*
(1965), a single pattern predominates: Within a womblike
room rather ordinary people pursue their rather ordinary business; a mysterious figure enters, and the commonplace room
becomes the violent scene of their mental and physical breakdown. Whether Pinter is dealing with a triangular situation
among the lower class, as he does in the early plays, or with
the better-educated, better-heeled middle class, his focus
most recently, this womb-room, expulsion theme and its accompanying light-dark, dry-damp, warm-cold imagery establish the Pinter mode.

Such a pattern begs for symbolic interpretation. Is this the
existential dilemma being replayed — man both seeking order
in an orderless universe and confronting the chaos that ultimately overwhelms him? Is it a reworking of Heidegger's "on-
tological insecurity" — man clinging to the room that offers
identity and safety in a world commanded by strange and
unkind gods? Or are the plays poetic images of man's efforts
to communicate in the absence of a fixed system of reference?

Any of these overviews, which Pinter's critics have been

prone to adopt, has an appeal because it seems to explain material that is often obscure and seemingly symbolic and philosophical. It gives one a sophisticated handle for dealing with Pinter and places the author in line with many of his contemporaries in the so-called Theatre of the Absurd. But Pinter insists: "I feel very strongly about the particular, not about symbolism. People watching plays tend to make characters into symbols and put them up on the shelf like fossils. It's a damned sight easier to deal with them that way." To "tie things up, to be explicit," he continues, is a "conspiracy" against "the texture of living."

Certainly, as Pinter intends, his characters come to life. They have a dramatic force that depends upon the vividness with which the heart of their emotional life is laid bare, rather than the manner in which they symbolically represent philosophical dilemmas. Pinter is not primarily a symbolic or philosophical writer. As a matter of fact, he is not particularly concerned with large metaphysical issues. Although questions about ultimates and absolutes may be abstracted out of his plays (as such truths are contained in all great art), there is something more immediate and essential in his work that resists allegorical or philosophical categorization.

Pinter does not offer Beckett's sad but grandiose perspective of an Everyman on the road of life, awaiting and confronting larger forces. Instead, Pinter focuses upon an Everyman who exists in his ordinary activities at home or at work, making the seemingly insignificant decision to eat cornflakes for breakfast, contending with the threat of a cold, and combating a bee in his morning tea — confronting the muted emotional turmoil of everyday life.

There is a joke in which a woman says, when asked who makes the important decisions in her marriage: "My husband does. He decides what to do about Vietnam, the race problem, and the cold war. I make the small decisions: which house to buy, what neighborhood to live in, what friends to choose."

The ironic truth of the joke is Pinter's. The emotional chaos of our lives is not a disorder born of cosmic or political confrontation but rather the product of our daily conflicts. This is the Pinter matter: the manner in which one lives from day to day, unaware of and unconcerned with moral and, above all, metaphysical issues; the way in which men actually spend their time considering what to have for dinner rather than contemplating eternity; the way in which loneliness and despair are immediate problems resulting from unhappy experiences with family, friends, and job, rather than the consequences of one's metaphysical discomfort in an alien universe.

Psychologists have long noted that, in the communication between people, the rational verbal interchange is only the most superficial facet of a multilevel communication. Eric Berne, in his recent book *Games People Play*, gives common examples of these games of *double-entendre*, where the second level of meaning may be emotional, illogical, and unconscious — often opposed to the first. What Pinter reveals in his plays, as Berne illustrates in his more formal study, is how the daily routines and habitual interchanges between intimates are neither as simple nor as innocent as they seem. In fact, the purposes of banal conversation are often quite sinister, for beneath the spoken word, beating with an unheard but emotionally palpable potency, are the sensual, violent, and often cruel impulses that are the real life of man. The patterned words are a ritual that protects; they are the religion of everyday life.

Pinter has been justly praised for his faithful reproduction of the nuances of ordinary speech, for his impeccable recording of its hesitations, repetitions, and incoherences. More precisely, what Pinter mirrors is the manner in which language disintegrates as internal impulses threaten and the speaker grows less assured of his patterned behavior. It is here that Pinter's linguistic mastery lies. As he charts the faltering of word games, he measures the increase of verbal wastefulness, the pointedness of clichés, the preponderance of *non sequiturs* in word and deed, and the punctuating and final silences. Ultimately in Pinter's work, the disintegration of normal language becomes a measure of dramatic tension, and, in a sense, drama exists at the level of language, as opposed to plot. In effect, exposition, crisis, and denouement are marked by verbal congruity, dissolution, and final resolution.

Pinter comments upon the manner in which we manipulate words, the significance of silence, and his task in coping with ordinary language:

> The speech we hear is an indication of that which we don't hear. It is a necessary avoidance, a violent, sly, and anguished or mocking smoke screen which keeps the other in its true place. When true silence falls we are still left with echo but are nearer nakedness. One way of looking at speech is to say that it is a constant stratagem to cover nakedness . . .

and,

> People fall back on anything they can lay their hands on verbally to keep away from the danger of knowing and of being known.

Pinter even admits, paradoxically for a dramatist: "I distrust words. What I feel about them is almost a kind of nausea." Yet it is with the fine edge of language that Pinter cuts through the verbal apparel by which man hides his naked, often vicious, reality. His work is a careful carving of the truth of character beneath the stratagem of words.

This paradox explains part of the Pinteresque, but it still leaves unaccounted for one essential ingredient — the mysterious, grotesque menace, that element of the bizarre, the extraordinary, the seemingly unreal, which always intrudes and disrupts Pinter's people somewhere about the middle of a play — for example, the blind Negro, Riley, in *The Room*, or the deaf, almost blind matchseller in *A Slight Ache*. Since these characters seem to be unrelated to the people visited and, therefore, external figures of some kind, they are often interpreted as the gratuitously malign forces of the universe, the inexplicable terror of the Absurd.

On closer examination, however, these "menacing figures" are not menacing at all. If anything, they are benign and virtually indifferent observers upon the scene. The blind matchseller on the road, for example, presents no threat to the comfortable bourgeois inhabitants of the country house, just as Goldberg and McCann in *The Birthday Party* are simply two businessmen visiting a seaside resort. Nevertheless they, like the matchseller, lead to calamity within a seemingly serene situation. As we shall see, however, the calamity provoked stems from the totally irrational responses to these men.

In effect, the so-called victimizers are merely screens onto which are projected the primitive and repressed feelings of the victims, heretofore submerged by the games. If any destruction occurs on stage, it is due to the would-be victim's enactment of his own hidden violence. In a sense, the menacing figures are Pinter's technique for leading his characters into exposing themselves.

The pattern is simple: The "intruder's" appearance initiates the breakdown of the patterned words and games, the habitual stratagems to cover nakedness. It also challenges the serenity and security provided by the room, whose arbitrary structure in effect parallels the habits of word and deed. At last, as the internal menace is fully projected externally, language disintegrates, and the so-called victim is expelled from the room; he finally exhibits himself in all his mental nakedness.

Like many of the other moderns who break with traditional form, Pinter evokes a perplexing variety of emotional responses from his audience. On the one hand, he arouses a mixture of laughter and contempt as he appears to mock the manners (games) of his characters. On the other, he often draws us into an intense sympathy with these people who, in their struggle with what seems to be a nameless and overwhelming terror, are not so unlike ourselves. One is caught between laughter and terror as he witnesses the horrific and hilarious discontinuity between what man says and what he is.

In regard to the terror, one wonders about the extent to which this theater approaches tragedy and is provocative of the classic responses of pity and fear. Certainly in watching Edward's brutal submission (*A Slight Ache*) and Rose's final blindness (*The Room*), one is deeply moved by these people who suffer from a fate they cannot control. Our pity and fear, in effect, are due to our realization that man may as easily be cut down by unknowable and uncontrollable inner forces as by the more traditional supernatural machinery, that the psychological concretizations of one's inner chaos may lead to calamity as surely as the gods descending from Olympus.

Yet Pinter's characters are far from tragic, for a number of reasons, an essential one being their lack of that dimension of the human spirit, that final moral strength, which allows the tragic hero to overcome through commitment and ultimate insight. Ordinary men in every way, Pinter's characters choose only to measure out their lives in their room. Should the internal furies threaten, they would, if they could, find another room or game in which to hide. That they ultimately face expulsion and exposure has nothing at all to do with their choice within the scheme of things.

The comic element in Pinter predominates, as the author lampoons the banal clichéd banter revered in the word-games played in the lives of the educated and uneducated, as well as in those of the rich and poor. Pinter brings to life the everyday silliness of Everyman and in so doing is uncannily funny. Yet he does not rely upon traditional devices of exaggeration for comic effect; this he achieves by a deadly precision of representation. It is as though Pinter is saying that, if one looks into his neighbor's kitchen and merely observes what happens, one will be amused.

What is extraordinary, however, is that although many of his over-all effects seem akin to those of traditional comedy or satire, Pinter's target is neither human foibles nor social institutions. Instead, Pinter lampoons the contract made *between* man and society. One may well question the propriety of the terms *comedy* and *satire* in discussion of Pinter's plays, for both would seem to demand that their target be correctable, whereas the absence of any standard (and the affirmation it implies) marks Pinter's work. Nevertheless, a single and conspicuous subject is under persistent attack.

Edward, in *A Slight Ache*, is not unlike Pinter's other men, although he plays the role of refined academician. By profession he is an anthropologist, by avocation a humanitarian who professes a concern and kindness for all living things: Edward has devoted a large portion of his life to the study and cultivation of various species of flora and fauna. Yet, the appearance of a wasp near his morning marmalade, no less than that of a sick, old, and debilitated man on the road behind his house, stirs his rage, and he bullies and beats both. Teddy, in *The Homecoming*, is another academician who holds the respect and admiration of his colleagues and family. But, like Edward, Teddy's expertise in the humanities cloaks a basic violence toward human life. Again and again, Pinter's characters profess the social niceties or demonstrate their sophisticated expertise, as the dramatist wields his unrelenting whip and strips them down to their essential, brutal, and irrational selves.

Pinter's indictment is enormous, though he attacks neither the particular society that forces its Edwards and Teddys into their precariously patterned lives nor the individuals who select their particular roles. Given any society and any role, Pinter's conclusions would remain the same: Man is a rather untidy creature who must, and yet cannot, live within the ostensibly tidy company of men.

Pinter's assault is leveled at the sources responsible for this terrible disparity between one's acts and impulses — civilization itself. All societies, he seems to be saying, have taught that one must repress his deepest feelings, for once they force themselves into actual behavior, they are vile and irreversible. In effect, Pinter condemns the initial contract that man makes with society, the unmanageable, indeed unworkable, negotiation of man and *all* institutions. Civilization, he seems to say, may well be necessary, but one must question the expense of spirit that goes along with the bargain.

The same can be said when one compares Pinter with many of his contemporaries in their Theater of Social Protest. Although Pinter's attack includes contemporary society, his critique, as we have said, is not limited to a particular class or set of institutions; his target is at once less specific and more inclusive than, say, John Osborne's. Unlike the social realists, Pinter aims at all social forms and at the shackles and misery that are man's inevitable lot when he enters into the company of other men. Pinter's aim is really, as Freud's was, "Civilization and its Discontents." There is something about the nature of the individual that is incompatible with the communities of men.

Comedy, satire, social criticism, and tragedy, despite their many differences, share at least one common element. They embody a standard of behavior, a measure against which we can determine the potential of man — either in a social or cosmic framework. Although Pinter mirrors what man is, he never judges his characters. He suggests no alternative for their foolishness, just as he denies their realization of any human potential. One never senses, in Pinter's work, the limits of being, the lost or potential truth possible to the human spirit. Pinter again maintains the impossibility of absolutes and final judgments:

The desire for verification on the part of us all, with regard to our own experience and the experience of others, is understandable, but cannot always be satisfied. I suggest there can be no hard distinctions between what is real and what is unreal, nor between what is true and what is false. A thing is not necessarily either true or false; it can be both true and false.

At this point, let us consider Pinter's theater and the Absurd. It is tempting to say that the mysterious intruders in the plays are Godots-arrived (The Eternal Nothing), and that Pinter's characters embrace them and then continue the process of living with the clarity and scorn of Camus's Sisyphus. But one must question this explanation.

First of all, Pinter's heroes, unlike Camus's or Sartre's, are ordinary men, and it never occurs to them to scorn the second coming, to admit that no revelation is, or ever will be, at hand. Second, even if they were, as Camus would say, to realize their absurd freedom and, as Sartre puts it, to choose their lives, any "engagement" would be a self-delusion, since, within the Pinter world, one's acts are ultimately determined by inner forces rather than rational choice. Finally, given the remaining alternative, one doubts that Pinter would even want his Stanleys and Alberts to strive willingly to understand the violence that rules them. Unlike Beckett, who looks at this matter of self-knowledge with as sympathetic and sober an eye as Sophocles or Shakespeare, Pinter would seem to insist that no advantage comes of acknowledging the divided sensibility.

To question the "Absurd" nature of Pinter's work requires additional definitions of this elusive term. Ionesco's "Absurd" demands a dramatic rendering of both material and spiritual worlds. Pinter, however, not only ignores the spiritual dimension, but he also retains elements totally antipathetic to Ionesco's drama: normal time sequences, traditional elements of plot measured in time and space, and realistic, syntactically ordered language.

If one measures Pinter's work against Martin Esslin's notion of the "Absurd" (coined in *The Theatre of the Absurd*), he has only to repeat that Pinter's characters do not exist on what Esslin calls "the edge of being," alone in the universe as they confront the very problems of existence. Instead, they are active in their everyday capacities, unconcerned with ultimate realities, rather than willfully ignoring them. Furthermore, if one looks to the source of Esslin's label, Camus's hero in "The Myth of Sisyphus," one must totally reject Esslin's "Absurd," since, if Pinter's figures are not concerned with ultimates, they surely lack the scorn, triumph, and nobility that exalt Sisyphus as he bravely commits himself to eternally rolling the rock to the top of the hill — in spite of an ultimate meaninglessness. One cannot say of the Pinter protagonist, as Camus so eloquently sings of Sisyphus: "He is happy."

If Pinter's work is absurd, it is so only in the most ordinary sense of the term. His characters face two alternatives: either they can remain in their rooms and play their routine games of living to avoid the onslaught of forces they care not to question (Teddy, *The Homecoming*), or, despite their efforts to the contrary, they may be met head on by these vicious energies, in which case they must be reduced to literal insanity (Aston, *The Caretaker*) or to the state of a babbling animal (Stanley, *The Birthday Party*).

What is of crucial importance is that Pinter is neither an existentialist nor an absurdist, for he never portrays the existential dilemma wherein man seeks an order in an orderless universe. Pinter is simply, if a label is necessary, a ruthless realist. His characters face not so much disorder in the universe as disorder in themselves. They try constantly to structure their lives, but, unaware that their actions and behavior revolve around deeper sources than conscious ones, they are constantly confronted by chaos. But again, this is a disorder of the self, not the universe.

It is virtually impossible to categorize Pinter's work for, although echoes of Beckett and Ionesco (and even Pirandello and Mallarmé) remain, Pinter is a very different writer from his contemporaries. One can speak only of influences, although Pinter has well transformed his borrowings — from Chekhov's haunting banalities to Kafka's mysterious intruders — into his own unique statement. Perhaps, however, Pinter has learned most from Alfred Hitchcock, since, like this elder statesman of black humor, Pinter has created a form out of carefully measured and evocative pauses, as well as comic and horrific sequences.

Basically, the tradition to which Pinter is most akin is that of the modern exploration of the underside of self and the complexities of thought. In a sense Pinter has attempted in dramatic form what writers such as Virginia Woolf and Joyce have accomplished in the novel. He has tried to realize dramatically the complexities of consciousness and the irrational welter — "the seething cauldron," as Freud named it — that lies beneath it. This is a grand attempt, considering the inevitable limitations that the dramatic form places on an exposition of interior self.

The Room begins with a lengthy monologue as the faded, sixty-year-old Rose scuttles about her one-room flat and talks to her silent husband, fifty-year-old Bert Hudd. She speaks mostly of ordinary matters — the weather, Bert's breakfast, and their comfortable room. When Mr. Kidd, the landlord, enters, the banal monologue becomes a banal dialogue, punctuated by Kidd's seemingly irrelevant recollections of his sister's "lovely boudoir" and his mother's Jewish background. Bert and Kidd depart, and a young couple enters. Told by a mysterious man in the damp and dark basement that this room is vacant, Mr. and Mrs. Sands inquire after the landlord, but they are uncertain of both his name and whether or not they have just come up or down the stairs. Much equivocation follows: How can Rose's room be to let if she lives in it? When Kidd returns, his only consolation for Rose is that a blind Negro named Riley waits in the basement to speak to her. Angry because she knows neither Riley nor any other strange man, she initially forbids his visit but then encourages it. Riley enters, only to submit to Rose's sadistic verbal attack. He then calls her Sal, presumably a childhood name, tells her that he has a message from her father, who wants her home, and Rose relents. Bert returns, after driving his van through the cold and ice, and speaks for the first time in the play. He boasts of his day, after which he mercilessly beats the Negro. Rose is struck blind.

The first few minutes of the play well illustrate Pinter's technique, in which meaning and communication depend more upon the connotations of language than its denotations, upon the emotional affect generated through and beneath the words and pauses. Rose ritualistically performs her daily routines, but her monologue — about trivia — reveals that her fears of the cold, the basement, foreigners, or even unsatisfactory rashers, are projections of an internal terror. The word *it* and the references to the weather act like condensed dream images and refer not only to external reality but to Rose's mental turmoil as well. In saying, "You might as well have something inside you," Rose concretely defines her emotional predicament. Perhaps one may fill the void of daily activity with games and that of the inner life with food. What Rose must avoid, at all costs, is the upset that the cold, damp, hunger, foreigner, or Negro would provoke within her room. Any of these would be, as she concretely says, "murder," while Pinter begins his equation of these externals and Rose's unconscious.

This'll keep the cold out. . . . It's murder. . . . You eat that. . . . You can feel it in here. . . . I wouldn't like to live in the basement. . . . No, this room's all right for me. I mean, you know where you are. When it's cold, for instance. . . . Who lives down there? . . . Maybe they're foreigners. . . . If they ever ask you, Bert, I'm quite happy where I am. . . . Nobody bothers us.

To ensure her safety, Rose plays a complicated game. Like most of Pinter's women, she is the wife-mother-bitch, not only to Bert, but to the other men who enter her room. She infantilizes, emasculates, and then plays the coquette with each.

She is, at first, the overprotective mother: She butters Bert's bread, feeds him milk, and warns: "You'd better put on your thick jersey"; she even dresses him. Bert, to be sure, is portrayed as a silly boy. He wears a ridiculous hat and reads a comic book. Virtually mute until the end, he is reduced to the level of a child, too infantile to speak.

Rose is also castrating. The tea, like other objects in the play, takes on concrete meaning as Rose identifies its strength with her domineering role and Bert's passivity. She offers Bert "nice weak tea. Lovely weak tea. . . . Drink it down," but she says of hers, "I'll wait for mine. Anyway, I'll have it a bit stronger." As additional objects gain concrete psychological meaning, Rose more vigorously emasculates her husband. Kidd, for example, has warned of the icy roads, but Rose picks up his identification of the sexual with Bert's van and she brutally castrates Bert in four short words. Pinter is a master of *double-entendre*:

> KIDD: . . . Still, you know how to manipulate your van
> all right, don't you? Where are you going? Far?
> Be long?
> ROSE: He won't be long.

Rose plays the same game with her landlord, whose name is as much a concretization of his mental state as Bert's physical appearance. The game has certain modifications, however, for Rose's sexual innuendoes and attack must be more guarded with a man who, after all, is not her husband. Hence, in what appear to be two separate monologues, seemingly tangential materials are paralogically related as Rose and Kidd talk in a kind of associative manner. Again, communication depends upon the connotations of language, upon the emotional and primal intimations beneath the words:

> ROSE: Why don't you sit down, Mr. Kidd?
> KIDD: No, no that's all right.
> . . . .
> ROSE: Don't you have a help? [*sic*]
> KIDD: Eh?
> ROSE: I thought you had a woman to help.
> KIDD: I haven't got any woman.

Kidd — the first "intruder" in Rose's room — tries to divert the conversation to less threatening matters, as he questions if the rocking chair is Rose's or his. He uses an oddly appropriate word as he progresses toward that degree of castration that Rose desires: "I could swear blind I've seen that before." But Rose will not relinquish her attack: "I thought your bedroom was at the back. . . ." Kidd fights participating: "I wasn't in my bedroom"; nevertheless, he succumbs to her command to sit down and reveals, in the metonymy of his response, the unconscious level upon which this battle is being waged: "I will sit down for a few ticks."

Rose resumes her cross-examination, and as Kidd weakens, she castrates him even more by now boasting of her husband and displaying his masculinity as if it were her own:

> ROSE: When was this your bedroom?
> KIDD: A good while back.
> ROSE: . . . I was telling you how he could drive.

14

Kidd tries to recover some trivial chatter, but his comments and odd associations reveal his erotic attachment to his sister:

> She was a capable woman. . . . Took after my mum . . . a Jewess. She didn't have many babies. . . . She used to keep things in very good trim. And I gave her a helping hand. . . . She always used to tell me how much she appreciated all the — little things — that I used to do for her. . . . She had a lovely boudoir. A beautiful boudoir.

After boasting through masked niceties of their separate sexual victories, Rose and Kidd finally come together in an emotional understanding. Their last two statements are pungently concrete:

> ROSE: What did she die of?
> KIDD: Who?
> ROSE: Your sister.
> (*Pause.*)
> KIDD: I've made ends meet. . . . Oh yes, I make ends meet.
> ROSE: We do, too, don't we, Bert?

This aggressive-mother-lover / passive-child-husband relationship is echoed when the second "intruders," Mr. and Mrs. Sands, enter. But the young Mrs. Sands is less successful in the role of castrator than Rose. There is every indication, however, that Mrs. Sands will mature to Rose's level of competence. In a sense, Rose confronts, in the Sandses, a mirror image of her own marital situation thirty years prior, when she and Bert searched for their room.

It is now Mrs. Sands who complains of the damp and dark, and she repeats Rose's "It's murder out." The young woman explains that she is looking for the landlord, whom she erroneously but curiously calls "Toddy," the baby name by which she addresses her husband. She too infantilizes all men. She approaches her husband in exactly the same way Rose has

15

Kidd: She demands that he sit down. Mr. Sands submits, although he fights to retain the rule of the roost:

> MRS. SANDS: You're sitting down!
> MR. SANDS (*jumping up*): Who is?
> MRS. SANDS: You were.
> MR. SANDS: Don't be silly. I perched. . . . You did not
> see me sit down because I did not sit bloody well
> down. I perched!

Yet, in her misinterpretation of his next, logical question, "Who do you take after?" she indicates some awareness of her maternal role, although she simultaneously reaffirms it by standing up: "(*Rising*): I didn't bring you into the world." Mr. Sands also realizes her domineering position: "Well, who did then? That's what I want to know. Who did? Who did bring me into the world?" Despite his infantilized role, Mr. Sands understands better than Bert (or Kidd) his wife's psychological needs and how real is her fear of internal darkness.

As they announce the reason for their visit, Rose grows increasingly more threatened: "You won't find any rooms vacant in this house. . . . This room is occupied." Rose's entire life has been an attempt to lock herself in this room, to have it function as an internal defensive system and as a support in her games with Bert. Hence her terror mounts as each intrusion offers to expel her and bring her closer to herself. Pinter plays with the equation of the basement and the unconscious, and the attack upon Rose gains graphic concretization as Kidd and the Sandses arrive from both upstairs and downstairs. Rose has yet to meet the visitor from the basement. Mr. Kidd becomes his emissary.

Rose welcomes Kidd, for she thinks he will inform the Sandses that her room is unavailable. But his return proves more alarming than consoling. In their previous encounter, when Rose viewed him as a threat, he became her prey. Now she would meet him upon the same grounds, but Kidd has astutely observed the Sandses' effect upon her. Rearmed, he can retaliate at precisely that level at which her games preserved her with him, but which the Sandses have already weakened: her control and security within the room:

ROSE: What did they mean about this room?
KIDD: What room?
ROSE: Is this room vacant?
KIDD: Vacant?

Kidd, whose stability is also precarious, has been sorely disturbed by the stranger downstairs, and, since Rose's defenses seem threatened, he can say: "You'll have to see him. I can't take it anymore. . . . Why don't you leave me be, both of you?"

In depicting this last intruder as a blind old Negro named Riley, Pinter creates a kind of surrealistic image that condenses the terrifying experience or emotion that Rose has known. Such a concrete yet suggestive dream symbol allows his audience to project onto it all of its own associations with lurking violence or dark, damp, blindness, and cold. Riley, a kind of emasculated superman, becomes the logical conclusion to each of the incremental threats imposed thus far by Rose's several visitors. Rose's reaction to him is, of course, the play's climax. In the few minutes before she meets him, she tries to regain some control. When he finally enters the room, she embraces the same aggressive role that has proved so successful with her other victims. Explicit now, however, is her basic anger and hatred toward all men:

You're all deaf and dumb and blind, the lot of you. A bunch of cripples.

Frustrated that Riley remains silent, her even more sadistic energies emerge. If she has subtly brutalized her husband and Kidd and enjoyed Mrs. Sands's emasculation of her husband, she now openly scathes the polite Riley: "My luck. I get

17

these creeps come in, smelling up my room. What do you want?" At Riley's response: "I want to see you," she continues:

> Well, you can't see me, can you? You're a blind man. An old, poor, blind man. Aren't you? Can't see a dickey-bird. . . . I wouldn't know you to spit on . . .

Again Riley shows no change in mood or person. Clearly he functions not so much as an external character as the inevitable return of her unconscious, after the breakdown of her protective rituals.

The precise nature of Rose's guilt is uncertain. One suspects, however, from the nature of her games (that is, her choice of Kidd and Bert as partners) as well as her subsequent amorous attitude toward Riley, that it has to do with an early experience with her father — curiously enough, a mirror image of Kidd's with his mother-sister. As Riley calls her by her childhood name and says, "Sal . . . I want you to come home," Rose identifies him with her father and acts out the initial incestuous relationship, either real or fantasized, that has necessitated her life's games. She not only accepts Riley's: "I wanted to see you" with her "Yes . . . yes . . . yes," but she caresses his eyes, the back of his head, and temples.

Bert interrupts this intimate scene. That he is calm and self-possessed rather than violent, as one would anticipate, restores dramatic tension. He has been out in his truck all day: "I drove her down, hard. They got it dark . . . very icy out. . . . But I drove her." Language again operates on an evocative rather than rational level. Despite the dark and cold (he is finally outside of Rose's warm room), Bert has accomplished a sexual victory. He may at last answer Rose's: "Oh I know you can drive, can't you?" and Kidd's: "You know how to manipulate your van, don't you?" Bert boasts:

> I sped her. . . . She was good. . . . One [car] there was. . . . I bumped him. . . . I had all my way. . . .

18

> She was good. She went with me. . . . I use my hand.
> Like that. I get hold of her. I go where I go . . .

In some way, Bert has regained a semblance of virility (he "bumped" his rival and had his "way" with her). Now faced with a parallel scene in his room, Bert reasserts his masculinity in the only way he knows, blind violence; he "bumps off" Riley. Yet in so doing, he acts out a part of Rose's deepest wishes and ambivalence: He attacks the primal figure for her. Rose may emasculate men in games, but when she is drawn into life and fantasy becomes deed, she cannot tolerate the reality that has been created. Her guilt — not only from re-experiencing her buried feelings toward her father but also from acknowledging her everyday castration of males — is so great, she cannot witness the slaughter (the reality), and hence it is she who becomes blinded.

Several years after he completed *The Room*, Pinter said of Riley:

> Well, it's very peculiar. When I got to that point in the play, the man from the basement had to be introduced, and he just *was* a blind Negro. I don't think there's anything radically wrong with the character in himself, but he behaves too differently from the other characters; if I were writing the play now I'd make him sit down, have a cup of tea.

Pinter's humanization of the so-called menace marks an important aspect of his dramatic development. Not only is this figure less terrifying in the next few plays, but by *The Caretaker* and *The Homecoming*, Pinter omits him entirely and is able to give bolder emphasis to his subject: the struggle within the warring personality.

The Birthday Party begins much like *The Room*: a sixty-year-old couple talk of cornflakes, fried bread, and tea. Meg's role as wife-mother involves the two infantilized males in her house — her husband Petey, a deck-chair attendant, and their boarder, thirty-year-old, sloppy, and unshaven Stanley, presumably once a pianist but now retired to this decrepit house by the sea. For both Stanley and Meg, the boardinghouse is a haven of safety and security.

Into this homely retreat come two strangers: Mr. Goldberg, an apparently successful though overly talkative businessman, and his equally successful but more reserved colleague, Mr. McCann. After much seemingly banal conversation, it becomes apparent that the mere presence of the manic Goldberg and the depressive McCann will effect some violent displays among the house regulars.

As Stanley talks with Goldberg and McCann in Act II, his behavior grows more erratic. Stanley fears their presence as life-threatening. After a final confrontation, the strangers "demand justice" for Stanley's "sin," although its meting out is postponed until that evening, the occasion of Stanley's party, despite Stanley's insistence that it is not his birthday. One well anticipates the tone of the celebration, for Stanley has already accepted Meg's gift, a toy drum, and he has played it in an "erratic, uncontrolled . . . savage and possessed" manner.

The party is indeed a violent, primitive, sexual orgy. In the midst of games like blindman's buff, each character relives a fantasy of his troubled youth and, with the notable exception of Stanley, indulges in some sex play. As the scene ends, his glasses and drum broken, Stanley giggles at the prostrate Lulu and attempts to strangle Meg. Then, pinned and wriggling on the wall, Stanley receives the other characters who "converge upon him."

The final act recalls the first. Totally unmindful of the previous night's proceedings, Meg goes about her breakfast games. Stanley, however, has suffered some sort of nervous collapse and is about to be taken away by Goldberg and McCann, who also seem indifferent to the previous day's affairs.

Stanley enters, dressed in striped pants and top hat, but he is babbling. McCann and Goldberg promise to do everything for him, to make a man of him — or a woman. Petey offers a futile gesture to save Stanley, and the play ends as Meg prattles on about herself, the "belle of the ball" at Stanley's birthday party.

Pinter has often been compared with Kafka in his concern with the gratuitous assault of malign forces, but this may well be qualified by *The Birthday Party*. Kafka's K. does not know why the organization is after him, yet he seeks to understand both it and his own condition. Pinter's men, on the other hand, clearly understand both; Stanley feels a profound guilt for his former actions while he strives to escape any coming to terms with himself or his pursuers, although in so doing he reveals, in the manner of his games, the nature of his sin. Pinter's drama takes shape, unlike Kafka's, as it defines both its protagonist's internal sin and guilt and external crime and punishment.

Specific definition of Stanley's sin and crime is the subject of the play, but it can be stated briefly: In an effort to deny an amorous relationship with his mother, whereupon he usurped his father's place in the household, Stanley has moved to a new land and become the hopeful son of his present family. In doing this, however, Stanley has similarly and unknowingly displaced the present father to establish a lover-son relationship with his wife. Not until his confrontation with Goldberg and McCann does Stanley admit his sin and suffer a kind of internal purgation. *The Birthday Party* builds upon the Freudian interpretation of the Oedipus myth.

Pinter's introduction of Stanley as the son-lover and Petey as the emasculated husband reminds us of the beginning of *The Room*. Meg tells the diminutively named Petey that she has just served Stan his tea:

PETEY: Did he drink it?
MEG: I made him. I stood there till he did. I tried to get

21

him up then. But he wouldn't, the little monkey. I'm
going to call him. . . . Stan! Stanny! . . . I'm coming up to fetch you if you don't come down! . . .
One! Two! Three! I'm coming to get you. . . . Now
you eat up those cornflakes like a good boy.

Meg has a number of games that act to seduce Stanny into
eating, but they are complex, for they involve her repression
of sexual desire for him and his participation as a boy rather
than a man. The vain and egocentric Stan is willing and, he
thinks, capable of playing any game she demands to assure
his place in the room:

MEG: Was it nice?
STAN: What?
MEG: The fried bread.
STAN: Succulent.
MEG: You shouldn't say that word.
STAN: What word?
MEG: That word you said.
STAN: What, succulent — ?
MEG: Don't say it!
STAN: What's the matter with it?
MEG: You shouldn't say that word to a married woman.

Stanley fails to understand that Meg's real satisfaction in this
game demands his erotic participation. He has all he can do
to suppress his own sexual impulses in order to maintain his
mental equilibrium: "Well, if I can't say it to a married woman
who can I say it to?" Minutes later, after talking of other
things, Meg reveals her continuing preoccupation with the
emotionally packed word "succulent." What gives the scene
its pungence, of course, is that while Meg scolds Stanley, she
is at the same time titillated that he finds her attractive: "Go
on. Calling one that." But Stanley is still teasing: "How long
has that tea been in the pot?" Like Rose, Meg associates the
strong tea with virility, and Stan picks up the cue:

MEG: It's good tea. Good strong tea.
STAN: This isn't tea. It's gravy.
MEG: It's not.
STAN: Get out of it. You succulent old washing bag.

The sexual meanings beneath their word-games apparent and a moment of communication established, each fights against consciously expressing what is really on his mind by blaming the other for instigating his fear:

MEG: I am not! *And it isn't your place* to tell me if I am!
STAN: *And it isn't your place* to come into a man's bedroom and — wake him up.

The conversation returns to its banal pattern, but as Meg dusts the table, she "shyly" asks: "Am I really succulent?" and pursues the issue. Stan cannot deal with her approaches, and he violently replies: "Look, why don't you get this place cleaned up! It's a pigsty. And another thing, what about my room? It needs sweeping. It needs papering. I need a new room!" Stanley's outburst not only indicates his infantile relationship to Meg, in his demand that she keep his world well structured, but it also reveals his concrete hope that his mind will be clean if his room and the house are tidy. That Stanley's mind cannot be "cleaned up" will demand his final departure to a new room.

Meg understands Stanley, however, and if he is about to reject her, she can threaten his security and taunt him about the arrival of two new boarders. Her action recalls Kidd's sadistic threat after Rose humiliated him, and Stanley's reaction echoes Rose's: "I don't believe it." Stanley realizes Meg's defensive position, however, so he replies: "You're saying it on purpose."

But if Stanley looks to the room for comfort and merely plays along with Meg to retain it, he sometimes realizes that her verbal games and her needs to be his seductive mother are her only means of preserving her modicum of security.

He knows how to retaliate: He can pick up her threatening comments about the new boarders, treat them as though he believes them, and hence shock her into believing that *he* may leave her world:

> STANLEY: They're looking for someone. A certain person.
> MEG (*hoarsely*): No they're not!
> STANLEY: Shall I tell you who they're looking for?
> MEG: No.

Into Meg's and Stanley's precariously stable world come McCann and Goldberg, who conduct their own game of comradeship, one the leader, the other the follower. That they are such ordinary, seemingly stable and cordial men is so threatening to Stanley that he attributes his own vile motives to them and finally projects onto them all of his personal violence. Stanley thinks these nice men must see through him, and he concludes that they have arrived to punish him:

> STANLEY: I've got a feeling we've met before.
> McCANN: No we haven't.
> STANLEY: Ever been anywhere near Maidenhead?
> McCANN: No.

The sexual on his mind, Stanley makes the odd association of tea and then swiftly inhibits further thoughts about his childhood. His pauses are revealing:

> STANLEY: There's a Fuller's teashop. I used to have my tea
>   there.
> McCANN: I don't know it. . . .
> STANLEY: I was born and brought up there. I lived well
>   away from the main road.
> McCANN: Yes?
>
> (*Pause.*)

Too much anxiety provoked in this association of Maidenhead, tea, and childhood, Stanley returns to, "You're here on a short stay?" McCann is comfortable pursuing the social niceties, and he asks Stan if he finds the weather pleasant and what his occupation is. Stanley, as consumed by his private associations as Meg was with "succulent," confuses McCann's questions with his sinful past and questionable present and indicates his desire to escape:

> McCANN: You in business?
> STANLEY: No. I think I'll give it up.

Like a child, Stanley acts as though the adult McCann can see through his game; hence his immediate willingness to "give it up."

When Stanley hears voices from the back of the house — Goldberg has asked Meg if her husband is at home, and she has replied: "Yes, but he sleeps with me" — his harassment grows:

> You know what? To look at me, I bet you wouldn't think I'd led such a quiet life. . . . You know how it is . . . away from your own. . . . I'll be all right when I get back. . . . The way some people look at me you'd think I was a different person. I suppose I have changed, but I'm still the same man that I always was. I mean, you wouldn't think, to look at me . . . that I was the sort of bloke to — to cause any trouble, would you?

Stanley's confusion of the abstract and the concrete, his admission of the "trouble" he has caused, that he is "still the same man" he "always was," bespeaks his increasing and overwhelming guilt. As his guilt increases, he grows sadistic: This is "not a boarding house," he says, and he slanders Meg: "She's crazy." He finally grows violent with McCann in the outburst: "Listen. You knew what I was talking about before, didn't you?" The intrusion of Stanley's deepest thoughts into consciousness, as he strains to maintain normal conversation, provides the most tense moments thus far, but suspense mounts even further as Goldberg enters, another congenial chap who provides a shocking contrast to Stanley as he

25

talks, unthreatened, about youth and love. His platitudes about his happy childhood are intolerable to Stanley, who finally projects his own contradictory and nasty impulses upon McCann and Goldberg: "Get out. . . . You don't bother me. To me, you're nothing but a dirty joke." In an exchange of concretized emotional expression, which clarifies Stanley's crimes while it intensifies his guilt, he admits his control over Meg, the selfish advantage he takes of her games, and the diminished role into which he has forced Petey — his Oedipal triumph as a child and as a man.

Goldberg begins: ". . . Why are you getting on everybody's wick? Why are you driving that old lady off her conk?" and McCann, the other half of Stanley's internal debate, answers: "He likes to do it." Goldberg continues:

> Why do you behave so badly, Webber? Why do you force that old man out to play chess? . . . Why do you treat that young lady [Lulu] like a leper?
> . . . .
> McCANN: Why did you leave the organization?
> GOLDBERG: What would your old mum say, Webber?

Then Goldberg, repeating Stanley's earlier words, accuses the young man: "You're playing a dirty game." Again, with the equation of morality and cleanliness, Stanley is indicted: "When did you last have a bath?" His internal chorus, Goldberg and McCann, continue:

GOLDBERG: Don't lie.
McCANN: You betrayed the organization.
. . . .
GOLDBERG: Where was your wife?
. . . .
   What have you done with your wife?
McCANN: He's killed his wife.
. . . .
GOLDBERG: Where's your old mum?
STANLEY: In the sanatorium.

The details of Stanley's former life bear a striking resemblance to his present situation: His mother is in a sanatorium, and he now aims to drive Meg insane; he deserted or perhaps killed his wife, and he is similarly sadistic to his neighbor Lulu. The Oedipal son, Stanley is incapable of establishing a meaningful relationship with any woman; he has won his mother from his father, but he feels such guilt that he must punish all women.

Stanley's confession begun, the priests of his internal world continue: "What is your name now?" and Stanley, who would want to be ordinary and clean, cries out, "Joe Soap." Goldberg reminds him, however, that his purification is far from complete: "You stink of sin," because "You contaminate womankind. . . . Mother defiler. . . . You verminate the sheet of your birth."

Specific definition of McCann's and Goldberg's function is complex. As we have seen, they are less external forces — satanic messengers from the void or malign universe — than projections of Stanley's guilt, driving and uncompromising internal furies. Yet, they are externalizations not only of Stanley's guilt but also of his sin, two very different internal experiences, the first moral, the second instinctual. As they represent the first, they speak for the forces of society, the church, the "organization," the ruling system against which Stanley has sinned. Hence they accuse him of heresy, of sinning with Maidenhead, of driving his mother to a sanatorium, of abandoning his wife — and of reliving all of these events with his current family. That Pinter elaborates their function, however, demands that we examine the party scene, where they externalize instinct as well — not only Stanley's but also Lulu's and Meg's. In a sense, the party becomes a celebration of original sin and guilt in all men.

Acting as a kind of screen onto which each character's deepest impulses are projected, McCann and Goldberg bear witness to an orgiastic ritual. Meg, who dances in a dress her father gave her, is aroused to a frenzy in which she recalls her childhood and admits erotic fantasies toward her father. She identifies McCann with her father and pursues an affair with him. Lulu also reveals infantile and erotic fantasies toward her father, but she acts them out with Goldberg:

GOLDBERG: Lulu, you're a big bouncy girl. Come and sit on my lap. . . .
LULU: You're the dead image of the first man I ever loved.

As Goldberg "slaps her bottom" and says, "Where did you get this?" there follows:

LULU: My father gave it to me.
GOLDBERG: Maybe I played piggy-back with you.

Stanley is nearly insane as he looks on. In his trial, of just a few hours before, he admitted that his present life has been an effort to escape his first crime, the "verminating" of "his mother's sheets." Now, at a loss to pursue the games that have until now preserved his identity, Stanley is too paralyzed to play the party game — blindman's buff (a beautiful condensation of the life games this bluffing, would-be sexless, Oedipal male has pursued with Lulu and Meg). Yet, in admitting his guilt, he has been brought face to face with his sin and with those sexual energies that sent him to this boarding-house and necessitated his present life. These instincts released, Stanley, in horror, observes their enactment as McCann and Goldberg act out *his* own desires and conduct *his* affair with Meg and Lulu. Then, as if he had relived the first crime with his mother, his guilt becomes so overwhelming that he tries to relive the first experience completely: He tries to strangle Meg and assault Lulu. It is no surprise to the viewer when, at the end of the evening, Stanley becomes mute and must be carried away from this primal scene.

Stanley's dilemma — and this is at the heart of the play

and is true of all of Pinter's work — is that man is born with certain natural drives, and, as he grows up, he bears the burden of repressing what society then labels his illicit impulses. Unless he can do this, the Goldbergs and McCanns will erupt periodically to punish him for his original sin, his instinctual energies. The bind for man is that, if he acts upon his instincts, his deeds will terrify and haunt him; his only alternative is to attempt a constricting life out of the fear of what is inside. The great paradox is that what is inside is not simply the free and lusty energy, indulgence of which might at least bring pleasure, but the inhibitions of society as well. Guilt (the internalization of society) *and* the raw instincts live unhappily side by side. So it is that Stanley must be punished for the very energies he has sought to escape by leaving ordinary society.

The Birthday Party concludes on a profoundly bitter note. Pinter does not choose to end it as Stanley is led away; instead, he brings back Meg, who until this time has protected herself in games with Stanley. Now, however, pretending that he is still upstairs, she says: "Where's Stan? . . . Is he still in bed?" Not only has Stan been literally reduced to the level she has always desired for him, but her selfishness and self-delusion return. There seems to be no hope for Pinter's figures; a new game must be found.

Society's most violent members, its professional gunmen, are also victimized by internal forces. *The Dumb Waiter* wields an unrelenting humor and horror as it measures the incongruity of proud murderers playing games to avoid admitting what their lives are all about. Pinter omits his usual third-party intruder and introduces a mechanical dumb-waiter as the external barometer of his characters' inner turmoil.

As Gus and Ben await daily orders, in their basement room, they show the same concerns as most people. They read the newspaper and comment upon the unfortunate violence that occurs in the world, even to cats:

> BEN: A child of eight killed a cat.
> GUS: Get away.
> BEN: It's a fact. What about that . . . ?

They lament the absence of their afternoon tea, discuss the football season, make plans to attend a game after work, and talk about their room. Here are thugs who lead a dirty life but who demand clean sheets, and who, though in the business of murder, fear the damp and dark.

Part of their afternoon routine involves a kind of vaudeville sketch. Ben gives Gus some matches:

> GUS: Well, they'll come in handy. . . . Won't they?
> BEN: Yes, you're always running out, aren't you?
> GUS: All the time.
> BEN: Well, they'll come in handy then.
> GUS: Yes.
> BEN: Won't they?
> GUS: Yes, I could do with them.

Even in their two-bit routines, Pinter captures their precarious emotional life. Gus plays the fall guy with the matches, but he is also "always running out" on the job. Ben can now keep his partner in tune with the matches, but later, when the games are over, he will have to substitute his gun.

The internal menace intrudes as the precision of their word-game degenerates:

> BEN: Go and light it.
> GUS: Light what?
> BEN: The kettle.
> GUS: You mean the gas.
> . . . .
> BEN (*his eyes narrowing*): What do you mean, I mean the gas?
> GUS: Well, that's what you mean, don't you? The gas.

BEN (*powerfully*): If I say go and light the kettle I mean
 go and light the kettle.
GUS: How can you light a kettle?

This banter proceeds until, "They stare at each other, breath-
ing hard," and finally:

BEN (*grabbing him with two hands by the throat, at
 arm's length*): THE KETTLE, YOU FOOL!
GUS: All right, all right.
(*Pause.*)

This obsession with the gas/kettle, as well as the damp room
and dirty sheets, masks their overwhelming fear of personal
destruction. Guilt-ridden because they are, after all, murderers, they *expect* to be punished at any time. It is, therefore, of
profound importance to them to say the phrase properly, to
react to the newspaper appropriately, and to find the w. c.
operating regularly, for, in so doing, the ritual of their words
and the magic of their acts and the objects around them may
testify to their inner order and prevent the suicide of their own
mental stability. (Whether or not murder and suicide are two
halves of a single coin is of interest.)

Curiously enough, in his questions about their past and future contracts, Gus, the more insecure partner, becomes Ben's
menace. Ben is the tough guy only on the surface, because it
never occurs to him to question his job. Growing increasingly more upset whenever Gus raises a potential problem,
Ben finally becomes violent. Gus admits his guilt, as he says
he would like to meet their boss, "There are a number of
things I want to ask him. . . . I've been thinking about the
last one"; but Ben's reply reveals his totally represssed guilt,
"Which last one?" As Gus reminds him, "That girl," Ben grabs
the newspaper to avoid the issue.

Their mental equilibrium is so precarious that the slightest
problem in their external world seriously threatens it: Why
can't they have their afternoon tea? Who does clean up after

a victim has been slaughtered? The major threat occurs when an envelope is thrust under the door with demands that exotic foods be delivered upstairs, via the dumb-waiter: "Two braised steak and chips. Two sago puddings . . .". They send their own stale food, but the orders become incredible: "Macaroni Pastitsio, Ormitha Macarounada. . ." . Tension mounts, not only because of the demands from above, but also because they have yet to decide who cleans up their slaughtered victims, what they can do about their damp room and dirty sheets, and why the w. c. is broken. Furthermore, Ben cannot handle Gus's questions: "You never used to ask me so many damn questions. What's come over you?"

They finally return to their ritual, ostensibly the same one that began the afternoon. One reads the paper, the other goes to the w. c., and they decide to rehearse their business conduct: How to murder someone:

BEN: When the bloke comes in —
GUS: When the bloke comes in —
BEN: Shut the door behind him.
GUS: Shut the door behind him.
BEN: Without divulging your presence.
GUS: Without divulging my presence.
. . . .

But Ben omits an important detail: Gus *must* take out his gun in self-defense, for the victim might also have a weapon. That Ben realizes his omission is clear in his contradictory response:

GUS: You've missed something out.
BEN: I know. What?
GUS: I haven't taken my gun out, according to you.

The tube connecting the dumb-waiter with the other floors announces the day's orders — to Ben. Already planning Gus's murder in this last routine, Ben now projects onto the tube his urgent need to expel Gus in order to regain some mental equilibrium. The play ends as Gus returns from the w. c. stripped of his gun, and Ben aims a revolver at him. The w. c. finally flushes.

Pinter's title, though ingenious, is misleading. Unless the author has carelessly misused two words instead of one, the *dumb waiter* cannot refer to the mechanical object, a single or hyphenated word. Questions then arise: Is the dumb waiter the master or the slave in the Ben-Gus relationship, and if so, which is which? Ben, in rationalizing his life completely and in destroying what he foolishly thinks is his external menace, Gus, is literally dumb or stupid. Yet Gus is more the dumb waiter for Godot in his insistence upon questioning everything. Perhaps each is the waiter, the servant, to his internal drives.

There are additional insoluble problems. In both *The Room* and *The Birthday Party*, much of the dialogue and action revolved around food, for the characters strove to fill an inner void in meal rituals. Is Pinter suggesting that Gus provokes Ben's anger by hiding the food from him? Or, is Ben uninitiated into the observation of these rituals, as he says: "Eating makes you lazy, mate. You're getting lazy. . . . You don't want to get slack on your job." An entirely new possibility is also suggested: Was Ben to have been the victim, rather than Gus, since their rehearsal of the murder scene indicates that the role of victim or victimizer is solely determined by one's possession of the gun?

Although Pinter leaves these questions unanswered, his theme — the commingling of banality and evil — is provocative. One recalls, for example, Hannah Arendt who also discusses, in *Eichmann and Jerusalem*, the banality of evil as she portrays Eichmann more as a petty bourgeois functionary than as a willful satanic murderer. As Pinter seems to agree, the murderer, both criminal and political, is not the classic comic-book or movie villain type, but, like the murderers of *In Cold Blood,* he is tormented, incapable of controlling himself, and in search of the cleanliness and emotional calm of a small room.

A Slight Ache enunciates the manner in which the highly sophisticated games of the well-educated are inadequate in warding off vicious sexual energies. Pinter returns to the pattern of *The Room* and *The Birthday Party* in introducing the third-party figure. Now a harmless, old, mute, almost blind matchseller, the mere existence of this dirty and silent foreigner within Edward's and Flora's comfortable and clean world proves a formidable threat. So uncontaminated do they want to remain from the world of emotional values associated with the old man that it is all the more shocking when, their games thrust aside, they later identify with him and project onto him their hideous and filthy undersides. The play traces the manner in which the matchseller comes to represent a separate screen for both Flora and Edward, as each projects onto him mutually incompatible drives. Edward comes to admit his sexual impotence and Flora her sexual frustration. By the end of the play, Edward changes place with the old man to become the silent matchseller, and the dirty old man becomes Flora's lover.

Edward's and Flora's game is new. It varies from chic chitchat to elegant gourmandizing. The academician Edward thrives on pedantic precision, and sophisticated Flora (in the old days "Fanny") acts as gracious wife but also castrating bitch:

> FLORA: Have you noticed the honeysuckle this morning?
> . . . .
> EDWARD: Is that honeysuckle? I thought it was . . . convolvulus, or something.
> FLORA: But you know it's honeysuckle.
> . . . .

34

Edward — you know that shrub outside the tool-
shed . . .

EDWARD: Yes, yes.

FLORA: That's convolvulus. . . .

EDWARD: Oh.

(*Pause.*)

I thought it was japonica.

The protection offered by their games is so precarious that
the slightest deviation from daily routine provokes "a slight
ache." Edward, the Pinter prototype who measures out his life
with coffeespoons, notices a wasp entering his marmalade
pot. One would think the wasp life-threatening, so defensive and even cruel is Edward's reaction. Obsessed that *he*
must control it, Edward says to Flora:

Don't move. Keep still. . . . Don't move. Leave it. Keep
still. . . . Give me the lid. . . . Give it to me! Now . . .
slowly . . . carefully . . . on . . . the . . . pot! Ha-ha-ha.

But as the wasp continues to buzz and Edward's malice
grows — he'll drown it, squash it, choke it, suffocate it, and
scald it — his eyes ache. That his control over the wasp indicates, in his mind, his control over his life and even his physical prowess, is apparent when he later says to the matchseller:
"I could pour hot water down the spoon-hole, yes, easily,
no difficulty, my grasp firm, my command established, my
life was accounted for. . . ."

Edward's initial reaction to the matchseller is peculiar:
"For two months he's been standing on that spot. Two months.
I haven't been able to step outside the back gate." Clearly,
there is no rational basis for his fear of the old man (or the
wasp), unless he attaches some private meaning to him (or
to it). Nevertheless, his rage increases whenever he thinks of
the old man, and his eyes become more irritated.

Edward goes into the scullery, rather than the study, to

pursue his latest research, "the dimensionality and continuity of space . . . and time."

FLORA: What are you doing in here?
EDWARD: Nothing. I was digging out some notes, that's all.
FLORA: . . . I thought you were writing . . . about the Belgian Congo.

. . . .

EDWARD: Never mind about the Belgian Congo.
FLORA: But you don't keep notes in the scullery.
EDWARD: You'd be surprised. You'd be highly surprised.

A concrete answer, Edward has indeed been burying himself for years. If he dredges up what has been carefully repressed until now — his work with the Belgian Congo has perhaps brought him too close to the heart of darkness — one may well anticipate the emotional display that will follow.

Edward's aches intensify as he asserts his masculine authority in an unlikely insult to Flora:

EDWARD: Get out. Leave me alone.
FLORA: Really Edward. You've never spoken to me like that in all your life.

But Flora would rather infantilize him:

Oh, Weddie. Beddie-Weddie . . .

Although his eyes grow more bloodshot, Flora persists. She mocks his fear of the "poor old man," and Edward, torn between his own sense of weakness and a residual need to retain control, says:

I shall not tolerate it. He's sold nothing all morning. . . . I've hit, in fact, upon the truth. . . . The bastard isn't a matchseller at all. . . . He's an impostor. . . . I intend to get to the bottom of it. . . . He can go and ply his trade somewhere else. Instead of standing like a bullock . . . a bullock, outside my back gate.

The key words are, of course, in the last line. Pinter's castrated males are fond of projecting their own condition onto other "bullocks." That Edward should also accuse the old man of bad business and of being an impostor foreshadows his final identification with him. Nevertheless, Edward is frightened by his own violence, and when Flora suggests they call the police, he rationalizes his own control of the situation: "I can't say I find him a nuisance." His ache increases.

Since Flora is attracted by Edward's reactions to the old man, and Edward feels guilty about them, they decide to invite the old fellow in. They question him about himself and his preferences for lunch, but his silence terrorizes them. He does not play their game: "We have goose for lunch. Do you care for goose? . . . Sit down, old man. What will you have? Sherry?" The more threatened by his silence, the more elaborately they construct their game: "Curaçao Fockink Orange? Ginger beer? Tia Maria? A Wachenheimer Fuchsmantel Reisling Beeren Auslese? Gin and it?" Surely there is some sound play intended.

Edward finds the old man's silence intolerable, and his monologue, replete with precise information about history, philosophy, and plant life, becomes punctuated with private reveries. He recalls a squire who had three daughters:

> Flaming red hair. . . . The youngest one was the best of the bunch. . . . Fanny. Fanny. A flower. . . . I write theological and philosophical essays. . . . You met my *wife*? Charming woman. . . . Stood by me through thick and thin. . . . In season and out of season. Fine figure of a woman she was, too, in her youth. Wonderful carriage, flaming red hair.

It is difficult to logically order this dreamlike dialogue, but Flora later admits a youth identical to that of Edward's Fanny. The red-headed Fanny may indeed be the faded Flora, in fact or in Edward's fantasized memory of his young wife. Their lives, now less passionate and more organized around games, have necessitated Fanny's change of name. As Edward has grown older, and "out of season," he has become more concerned with flowers than fannies.

Edward also projects his own professional corruption upon the matchseller: "Yes, I . . . was in much the same position myself then as you are now. . . . Tell me, between ourselves, are those boxes full, or are there just a few half-empty ones among them?" Edward also reveals his revulsion for women and his dependence upon the room for protection: "Nothing outside this room has ever alarmed me. You disgusted me [like] . . . Fanny, the squire's daughter. . . . In appearance you differ but not in essence."

Flora's reaction to all of this is interesting. Although one suspects that she encouraged the matchseller to stand near her house — she boasts to Edward of how she "nodded" to him — she now senses that his appearance is too threatening to her husband. It is one thing to have Edward grovel in his passivity but another to drive him to the point of nonfunctioning. Flora, despite her sadism, is no masochist; she would not give up her game. She boasts to Edward of *her* power to have the old man move on: "I can . . . make him . . . Edward." But the game has gone too far. Edward has already lost control of his identity. When she mentions his name, he says: "Stop calling me that." His exchange of role with the old man already begun, he now insists that it is the matchseller who has a severe ache in his eyes, who "can't see straight."

Flora has an opportunity to be alone with the old man, and she also undergoes a psychic transformation. Where Edward admitted his impotence, Flora acknowledges her passion. Initially, she identifies the matchseller with her first lover, as if trying to re-experience that first passion. (In an earlier comment to Edward: "No thanks to you I had a night of uninterrupted sleep," she hints of the absence of any sexual life with him.) She says to the matchseller:

> I've got a feeling I've seen you before. . . . Between our-
> selves, were you ever a poacher? I had an encounter
> with a poacher once. It was a ghastly rape, the brute.
> . . . Years later, when I was a Justice of the Peace for
> the county, I had him in front of the bench. . . . I ac-
> quitted him. . . .

She asks the old man if he has a woman, or likes and thinks
about women and adds: "I'm sure you must have been quite
attractive once." His silence stirs her: "Sex, I suppose, means
nothing to you. Does it ever occur to you that sex is a very
vital experience for other people? . . . (*Seductively*) Tell me
all about love." Yet, as mother-lover, Flora reveals her ambivalence towards sex. She finds the matchseller "repellent and
hideous" while "appealing" and "amusing":

> All you need is a bath. A lovely lathery bath. And a good
> scrub. A lovely lathery scrub. . . . It's me you were wait-
> ing for, wasn't it? . . . And you came and stood . . .
> at my gate, till death us do part.

Rocking in her chair (one recalls Rose's sexual gyrations in
her chair), Flora admits her preference for the matchseller to
her husband: "You're a solid old boy. . . . Not at all like a
jelly." And she continues: "I'm going to put you to bed and
watch over you. But first you must have a good wacking great
bath. And I'll buy you pretty little things that will suit you.
And little toys to play with." To be sure, although Flora wants
a man, she will infantilize and emasculate him just as she has
her husband.

Edward returns and cries out: "You lying slut. Get back
to your trough!" He then reveals in youthful reveries his present impotence, as each recollection of a past glory becomes a
comment upon his present inadequacy. In an almost homosexual way he then babies the old matchseller, whose silence
stirs Edward's intermittent outcries of violence. In very concrete language, Edward says:

> You look different in darkness. Take off all your togs, if you like. . . . God damn it, I'm entitled to know something about you! You're in my blasted house, on my territory, drinking my wine, eating my duck! Now you've had your fill you sit like a hump . . .

Desperately trying to reassert his masculinity, he makes one last attempt to deny each failure of his life: He boasts of his feats at cricket, his business acumen, his successful defense against personal and professional enemies, "feeling fit, well aware of my sinews . . . my aim was perfect . . . my command established" — but he finally cries out the sad truth of his present predicament: "My life was accounted for. . . . Did I invite you into this room . . . in order to determine your resemblance to — some other person?" Gaining no response to this last, intimate confession, Edward fully projects onto the old man his entire self-consciousness: "That's good for a belly laugh. . . . Let it out. . . . You haven't been laughing. You're crying. . . . You're weeping. You're shaking with grief. For me." And as *he*, Edward, sneezes, he makes one of his last statements: "Come, come. Stop it. Be a man. Blow your nose. . . . Pull yourself together." Though only moments earlier Flora had said of the matchseller: "He's dying," she clearly had Edward in mind as he, now almost totally debilitated, cries out about his "fever" and falls to the floor. To complete the identification, Flora transfers the matchseller's matchbox to Edward, who is now ill-sighted, deaf, and dumb, and she leads the other man — who has remained silent throughout but is now "extraordinarily youthful" — into the house.

The Caretaker traces a scurrilous old man's futile efforts to pit two brothers against each other in order to gain a secure place in their room. Pinter sets aside the specifically sexual and the bizarre and concentrates upon the difficulty of maintaining human relationships because of the self-interest that prompts most communication.

His title has moral as well as descriptive (nominative?) value. It refers not only to the old man Davies, who temporarily acts as Aston's and Mick's caretaker, but, more importantly, to the care each man must take of every other, the games that *must be* observed if minimal communication, respect, and affection are to be established among men.

Pinter has said that his characters avoid the "danger of knowing and of being known." But he adds:

> . . . there invariably does come a moment [when one says] . . . what he in fact means. . . . And where this happens, what he says is irrevocable, and can never be taken back.

The Caretaker builds upon the fragile moments when the irrevocable is spoken.

The brothers have established a working relationship: Each complements the other in mood and interest, and they seem to be two halves of a single personality. Mick, rational and bourgeois, thinks a great deal about profit, the future, and, when judging Davies, about recommendation papers and bank accounts. His ambitions are extravagant: He will convert this run-down flat into a penthouse with afromosia teak veneers, cork floors, and rosewood tables. Aston, on the other hand, has rejected Mick's sort of life — or it has rejected him. He has found it impossible to live within the restrictions, inhibitions, and demands of society, and he has undergone shock treatment. Now he can function predominantly as a man of feeling rather than reason. Yet, if it is seemingly paradoxical that the rational Mick live with dreams of grandeur, the emotional Aston lacks any illusions whatsoever. As his brother thrives on unrealistic schemes of building new things, Aston devotes himself to repairing old, broken ones — for examples, the toaster and the electric plug.

Davies, who enters their world, is one of Pinter's most complex characters. He plays his own game — that of the unfortunate Everyman, whose forsaken nature demands kindness and charity. Yet, by nature he is a liar and a bigot, and he cannot conceal the selfish, greedy, and possessive traits that mark him as an opportunist.

Davies fails to maintain a single pose, whose set of patterned responses would at least establish his identity among men. Pinter ingeniously characterizes him as a man who not only lacks identification papers but who is also uncertain as to whether his name is Davies or Jenkins, a man without roots:

> ASTON: Where were you born?
> DAVIES: What do you mean?
> ASTON: Where were you born?
> DAVIES: I was . . . uh . . . oh, it's a bit hard, like, to set your mind back . . . see what I mean . . . going back . . .

In a sense, Davies' two names correspond to his two-faced games, which in turn seem to reflect the different personalities of the two brothers. (He introduces himself as Davies to Aston, but as Jenkins to Mick.) Nevertheless, he becomes each brother's caretaker, while he takes no care of the games that may or may not have to be played to maintain his position. Mick and Aston alternately say to him: "What's the game?" "Who are you?" "You're a bloody impostor."

Davies' predicament arises from the fact that experience has taught him to be fearful of others, and yet he fails to realize that his present encounter, at least with Aston, is a challenge to his life's lessons. He is always on guard with Mick and Aston, as he projects onto them his own petty motives and profound suspicions:

> DAVIES: I better come with you.
> ASTON: Why? . . .

DAVIES: I mean . . . when you're out. Don't you want
me to get out . . . when you're out?

It is a curious situation because, on the one hand, Davies may well distrust Mick, who after all is not unlike him — both evaluate life as they think society dictates and believe that material possessions determine identity and status. On the other hand, Davies foolishly mistrusts Aston and is incapable of understanding why anyone should give him money and a room without demanding something in return. Davies abuses and humiliates the gentle Aston who has only responded, honestly and unquestioningly, to Davies' pose as the helpless old man. When Mick appears and promises better and perhaps more tangible profits, the fickle Davies can only take advantage of his new situation and permit his greedy nature greater breadth.

In his portrait of Davies, Pinter may well have in mind the Pozzo-Lucky relationship in Beckett's *Godot* or even Brecht's master and slave in *The Exception and the Rule.* That is, perhaps among certain men, only two moralities are possible, that of the slave and the ruler. As the servant enjoys his bondage and fights gaining freedom, Davies enjoys his role as society's exile and constructs ludicrous excuses for not proceeding to Sidcup to recover his papers — for instance, his black shoes have brown laces. On the other hand, once he dupes the brothers into giving him a significant place in the household, he conveniently forgets the needs of the downcast and acts as possessive and tyrannical as the society that has initially victimized him.

Regardless of their role-playing, Pinter's three men are lonely. They fear the slightest intrusion into their precariously established room, and, in a sense, each is always a potential menace to the other. This sort of free-floating fear of general upset gains concretization in their daily activities and preoccupations. Aston's attempts to patch up his broken mental world, for example, are projected externally in his efforts to repair the broken articles in his room. Slow in thought and speech, he also seeks order in a jigsaw puzzle, which will, as he says, "speed things up." Davies, on the other hand, is obsessed with cleanliness, as though a neat external world and physical body could purify and order his internal life. The old tramp is also prejudiced against "foreigners," "Blacks" and "Indians," and he projects onto them his own violent impulses. It is both humorous and frightening as he admits his profound fear that Aston and he might share a common bathroom with Blacks.

This sort of projection of states of mind onto external objects and people accounts for Davies' response when Aston tells him that, as caretaker, he will have to answer all inquiries at the house: "Well, I mean, you don't know who might come up them front steps, do you? I got to be a bit careful. . . . Any [Tom, Dick, or] Harry might be there." Davies' destructive impulses are apparent in his fears of death, his obsession that if he sleeps near the window he will be in a draft, or his concern that the stove might be leaking gas: "What about this stove, I mean . . . it's right on top of my bed, you see? What I got to watch is nudging . . . one of them gas taps with my elbow when I get up, you get my meaning?"

Davies' only real threat is Mick. The old man has just played the forlorn tramp with Aston, whose sympathetic and generous response has had no ulterior motive, apart from the desire for friendship. The two have actually communicated in a rather emotional way, although Davies has offered and welcomed the exchange of mutual feeling only because it promised Aston's favor.

Mick's sudden appearance is alarming. Aston, who has neglected to inform Davies that he has a brother who owns the flat, faces Davies' rejection. Davies, on the other hand, views any stranger as hostile, although it is Mick, despite his banal chatter and apparent social success, who is perhaps most threatened that Davies will upset his well-patterned life. Mick grows obsessed with one question: Who is this tramp in *his* house with *his* brother? To clarify the circumstances, he asks: "What's the game?" and, pursuing his own, he emits a barrage of banalities to get the old man off guard. He succeeds, but at the same time he reveals his own fear of Davies' potential power: The gap between his words and intention is so great, Mick forgets Davies' answers and contradicts himself:

MICK: What's your name?
DAVIES: I don't know you. I don't know who you are.
(*Pause.*)
MICK: Eh?
DAVIES: Jenkins.
MICK: Jenkins?

. . . .

What did you say your name was?

. . . .

You remind me of my uncle's brother.

. . . .

How do you like my room?

. . . .

DAVIES: This ain't your room. I don't know who you are.
MICK: You know, believe it or not, you've got a funny kind of resemblance to a bloke I once knew in Shoreditch. . . . What's your name?

In pursuing his ritual, Mick's anxiety increases:

Are you a foreigner? . . . You're standing in my house. . . . Let's have a bit of respect. . . . I think I'm coming to the conclusion that you're . . . an old scoundrel. . . . You don't belong in a nice place like this. . . . I could charge seven quid a week for this . . . three hundred and fifty a year. . . . That'll cost you eight hundred and ninety. . . . Say the word and I'll have my solicitors draft you out a contract.

And mentioning Pinter's favorite object of internal dread (*The Room, The Birthday Party*), he threatens the old man: "Otherwise, I've got the van outside."

Throughout this cross-examination, water drips from overhead into a bucket to punctuate the dialogue with constant reminders of Aston's presence, and as Aston realizes Davies' treason, he grows increasingly more intent upon fixing the broken toaster.

Yet Aston has gone out to recover a bag of old clothes that Davies presumably left behind. Aware that Davies values possessions, Aston thinks he will regain the old man's favor if he gives him something to wear to Sidcup. Although the bag is thrown around the room, tension lurks beneath the seeming slapstick. First of all, having tried to establish some credit with Mick, Davies is uncertain about how to react to Aston's kindness. Secondly, if Davies finds appropriate clothing in the bag, he will have to resign his position as outcast, and how then could he beg Aston's charity?

> DAVIES: Well, I don't know about these sort of shirts. . . .
> No, what I need, is a kind of shirt with stripes, a
> good, solid shirt, with stripes going down.

Aston understands Davies' emotional predicament, and he offers him the job as caretaker.

Mick returns, conscious of a plot against him, and plans his campaign to expel Davies. But he must somehow dupe the old man into abusing Aston so it is he who recognizes Davies' duplicity and rejects him from the room. In that way, Mick can seem innocent and resume his former relationship with Aston. Far more clever than Davies, Mick contrives a scheme: He will be Davies' friend: "I think we understand one another. . . . We just got off on the wrong foot," and he offers him a sandwich. Thoroughly seduced by such spontaneous kindness, Davies is ready to betray Aston:

MICK: . . . You're my brother's friend, aren't you?
DAVIES: Well, I . . . I wouldn't put it as far as that.

Mick continues in his appeal to Davies' opportunism:

MICK: . . . Can I ask your advice? I mean, you're a man
of the world.
DAVIES: You go right ahead.
MICK: . . . I'm a bit worried about my brother. . . .
You see, his trouble is . . . it's not a very nice thing
to say.
DAVIES: Go on now, you say it.
(*Mick looks at him.*)
MICK: He doesn't like work. . . . It's a terrible thing to
have to say about your own brother.

Davies fails to see that this is a veiled attack upon him, hardly
a brother but a tramp, and he swallows the Mick-finn completely and insults Aston:

DAVIES: Ay . . . I know that sort. . . . Well . . . he's a
funny bloke, your brother.
MICK: What?
DAVIES: I was saying, he's . . . he's a bit of a funny bloke,
your brother.
(*Mick stares at him.*)

Mick then echoes his brother's earlier: "How would you like
to stay on here, as caretaker?" But his proposal, unlike Aston's, is motivated by personal revenge, although clothed in
business terms. Rather than promise the old man a home or
friendship or even offer him the apartment key, as Aston has,
Mick demands references and discusses salary.

Aston is a witness to all of these negotiations. Incapable of
understanding Mick's game and yet anticipating Davies' de-
sertion, Aston reveals how his friends and even his mother
have forsaken him. Our sympathies are completely with Aston,
for even his fragile attempts to repair the torn objects of his
material world are now beyond his control. Pinter again in-

47

creases dramatic tension by juxtaposing Mick's pragmatic attitude and business schemes with Aston's emotional monologue on the terror and loneliness of a life without games:

> [In the hospital] . . . I told them . . . what my thoughts were. . . . [The doctors said] we're going to do something to your brain. . . . If we do, you stand a chance. You can go out . . . and live. . . . The trouble was . . . my thoughts . . . had become very slow. . . . I couldn't think at all. . . .

Aston's description of society's punishment to one who will not play its games is one of Pinter's most haunting speeches.

In the last act Mick succeeds in fully exposing Davies' duplicity, although Davies continues to take him at his word and to believe his place secure in the room:

> DAVIES: He's no friend of mine. You don't know where you are with him. I mean, with a bloke like you, you know where you are. . . . He's got no feelings. . . . You want to tell him . . . that we got ideas for this place.

Davies thinks it in his best interests to rid himself of Aston's affection, and so he brutally assaults him:

> . . . I'm not surprised they took you in. . . . You must be off your nut! Just keep your place that's all. Because I can tell you, your brother's got his eye on you. . . . I got a friend there. . . . They had you inside one of them places before, they can have you inside again. . . . Who ever saw you slip me a few bob?

Aston, shocked and exhausted, responds: "I . . . I think it's about time you found somewhere else." But Davies reminds him that, as Mick's caretaker, he can remain. Davies insults Aston's "stinking shed," and Aston responds, "You've been stinking the place out." Mick returns, and Davies puts his case before him. This is, of course, what Mick has been waiting for. With precise logic operative again, Mick begins the expulsion proceedings:

> MICK: What did he say then, when you told him I'd offered you the job as caretaker?
> DAVIES: . . . he said . . . he lived here.
> MICK: Yes, he's got a point. . . . I could tell him to go, I suppose. I mean, I'm the landlord. On the other hand, he's the sitting tenant.

They continue:

> DAVIES: I tell you he should go back where he come from!
> MICK: Come from?
>
> . . . .
>
> DAVIES: Well . . . he . . . he . . .
> MICK: You get a bit out of your depth sometimes, don't you?

Davies has gone too far. He doesn't understand that Mick is not only Aston's other half, but that he is also his brother's keeper.

Mick enumerates the absurd yet logical reasons why he doesn't want Davies to remain: "I want a first class experienced interior decorator. . . . You mean you wouldn't be able to decorate out a table in afromosia teak veneer, an armchair in oatmeal tweed and a beech frame settee with a woven sea-grass seat?" Mick gets at the old man now as though he had always accepted his word at face value, as though no other communciation were being established. He confronts Davies with an impeccable understanding of the entire situation:

> You're a bloody impostor mate! . . . You got two names. What about the rest? Eh? . . . What a strange man you are. . . . Ever since you come into this house there's been nothing but trouble. Honest, I can take nothing you say at face value. Every word you speak is open to any num-

49

ber of different interpretations. Most of what you say is lies. You're violent, you're erratic, you're just completely unpredictable. You're nothing else but a wild animal, when you come down to it. You're a barbarian.

The key words are, of course, "unpredictable," "erratic," and "barbarian." Mick speaks for Pinter in that to be human, or at least to deserve and maintain human contact, one must observe consistent games of conduct. Otherwise, one will be exiled from the community of men, as Davies will shortly realize, or he will be isolated within the irrational world of self, Aston's final condition. Mick has simply beaten Davies at his own game.

The final assault, however, occurs in Mick's next words, "And to put the old tin lid on it, you stink from arse-hole to breakfast time." Davies' continual gestures to protect himself have been in rituals of cleanliness. Thus, echoing Aston's earlier "You're stinking the place out," Mick concretely points the finger at Davies.

Although one is tempted to feel a certain pity for Davies at this point, Pinter prohibits it in allowing Davies a last gesture — which lays bare his well-deserved helplessness: his totally despicable, though futile, effort to regain Aston's favor. Davies now calls Aston friend, tells him he'll help build his shed, admits that he likes the shoes he had earlier scorned, and promises not to make any noise to disturb him. But the game is up.

This tendency toward a more direct rendering of character motivation follows in Pinter's television plays, *Night Out* and *Night School*. In the first, Pinter's familiar misogyny controls his portrait of a domineering mother-lover who resents her son's introduction into the normal world of experience. Although Albert ventures out to a party, hostile fantasies toward his mother as well as grotesque sexual acts provide his eve-

50

ning's entertainment. The night out becomes Albert's futile endeavor to escape the destructive possessiveness of his mother.

Three more television plays followed: *The Dwarfs, The Collection,* and *The Lover.* Len's comment in *The Dwarfs* — "The point is who are you . . . the scum or the essence?" — sums up Pinter's focus upon the young man's identity. Major questions reappear: Is life more tolerable if one hides behind socially accepted patterns of behavior ("Get a steady job. . . . [Be] a man."), or if one expresses and lives out his erratic inner compulsions?

The play traces Len's mysterious move from his London flat to a mental institution and how his thoughts are projected onto two other figures in the play, Mick and Pete. Len is preoccupied with an army of dwarfs who occupy themselves by eating rats, garbage, and human wastes and who then pile up their excrement with the other remains about them. Len calls the dwarfs "a brotherhood. A true community."

Although the play may well be an indictment of the violence inherent in the games people play, its rich verbal texture, condensed imagery, and lack of any plot coherence suggest its greater effectiveness in the novel form in which it was initially begun. Pinter says of the play, it "is apparently the most intractable, impossible piece. . . . Apparently, 99 out of a hundred feel it's a waste of time." Yet, he continues:

> The general delirium and states of mind and reactions and relationships in the play . . . are clear to me. . . . It's a play about betrayal and distrust. It does seem very confusing and obviously can't be successful. But it was good for me to do.

The Collection treats the multiple relationships that result when two couples meet — one heterosexual (James and Stella) and the other homosexual (Harry and Bill). James has accused Bill of an affair with his wife during a business trip, and although Pinter never indicates if the affair did in fact exist,

51

each of the characters confronts, accuses, and deals accordingly with each of the others in order to protect his vested interests — concretized in olives, cheese, vodka, and jazz.

Harry's jealousy, aroused when he meets Stella, is really due to his homosexual interest in Bill. James, who makes mysterious visits to Bill, browbeats him into admitting his guilt, but the two become chummy, suggesting that James has fabricated the initial charge because of his homosexual interest in Bill. Reversing the pattern, Bill visits Stella and forces her to admit her innocence, thereby reinforcing his possessiveness of Harry.

Again, as in *The Caretaker*, Pinter omits a concrete or fantastic portrayal of the internal menace and again demonstrates that the verifiable fact little matters — that is, whether James and Stella did have an affair. What is significant, rather, is the inner reality or personal meaning created by its possibility. Pinter has said, when asked if his couple spent an evening in Leeds: "I am not mystified. Basically I am not bothered. When an event occurs — some kind of sexual event in *The Collection*, for example — it is made up of many little events. Each person will take away and remember what is most significant to him. The more other people try to verify, the less they know."

The Lover is Pinter's least interesting play, as it diagrams multiple aspects of personality. More effective when he merely suggests the various dimensions of the fragmented mind, Pinter, in *The Lover*, oversimplifies a complex situation and draws two people who, in terms of psychological portraiture, are shadows by comparison with his other couples.

Richard and Sarah avoid Flora's and Edward's disaster (*A Slight Ache*) by acting out their sexual fantasies. It is as though they have a closet filled with disguises and scripts appropriate for different roles at different times of day. Richard plays faithful husband, lover, and rapist, while Sarah, at suitable times, is his faithful wife, prostitute- and whore-partner. Since each, in any of the roles, can freely express to the other his joy, jealousy, or anger about either one of his or the other's poses, each can protect both his and his partner's ordiary experience and fantasies. Pinter's point bears rementioning: Since the menace is internal, one can maintain a balanced life only if he unequivocably brings his fantasies to the surface and acts them out along with his rational, conscious wants.

The Lover is weak, for everything is overly spelled out. The tom-tom drum, high-heeled shoes, and Venetian blinds, whose functions change as the characters play their different roles, are heavy-handed, and — though a small point — Pinter even misleads us in his title, which ought, at least, to be pluralized, if not elaborated to *Lovers and Husbands and Rapists and Wives and Prostitutes, etc.*

If *The Lover* displays the acting out of fantasies, *The Homecoming* expands this subject with a finesse and ingenuity only suggested in Pinter's early work. The author not only draws his new husband and wife with brilliant insight, but he also develops to its fullest extent the relationship between homosexual males and heterosexual couples, significant in all of his earlier work (even in *The Caretaker*, if Mick and Aston are not really brothers).

The Homecoming again treats the struggle for power and sexual mastery beneath the ritualized games of daily life, yet it has a primitive quality, as Pinter reveals, both in action and imagery, the uncontrollable, bestial underside of man. Several struggles intermingle, but each is dominated by the commanding, castrating, and castrated father Max, who seeks control over his children, yet in many ways is controlled by them. Sons meet brothers only to reinforce their own or the others' homosexuality or impotence, and, finally, each of the men confronts the play's only woman who, in appealing to each as mother-lover-whore, reinforces their sexual plight.

The plot involves the arrival of Ruth and her academic husband Teddy at his father's all-male household. Ruth's appearance — this is the first time a woman has entered the house since Max lost his wife Jessie — brings to light the homosexuality of one son (Lenny) and the others' frustration and impotence. Observing Ruth's effect on the household, the father concludes that she must leave her husband and remain at the house as the family mistress. At the end of the play, the old uncle reveals that he observed one night, in the back seat of his cab, Jessie's infidelity with Max's best friend Mac, whom Max has always worshipped and held up to his sons as a moral and masculine example. At this point the uncle has a stroke, and Max kneels at Ruth's lap and cries: "Kiss me."

From the beginning of the play, the competition and hostility among the men is apparent. Max brags to his sons about his masculine superiority, and he also recalls his friendship with Mac — the curious similarity of names suggests not only a Cain-Abel brotherhood, but also a possible homosexual relationship. Like Bert (*The Room*), who brags of the "manipulation" of his van, Max tells of the great career he might have had as a horse-trainer. Then Lenny, imitating his father, boasts of his prowess with horses. But Max cuts him off with a curious choice of word and gesture that frightens the already well-emasculated boy:

LEN: You'll go?

. . . .

MAX: Will I, you bitch? (*He grips his stick.*)

Lenny, reduced to a whimpering child, punctuates his response with "Dad . . . Dad . . . Dad . . .". One senses that this dialogue and its accompanying gestures have been repeated many times, that this is a game or ritual enacted daily to maintain the *status quo* and the clarification of power

54

positions, for immediately following, Pinter creates a tableau-like effect with his stage directions: "Silence. Max sits hunched. Lenny reads the paper."

Sam, the uncle who witnessed but never disclosed Jessie's indiscretion, enters, and the struggle for control begins between Max and his brother. Sam offers a weak consolation to Lenny, as if to show he is familiar with the daily proceedings: "I'm here, too." But as Sam brags that he is "the best chauffeur in the firm," Max tries to emasculate him: "Why aren't you married?" The sixty-three-year-old Sam answers: "There's still time." Max's response: "Above having a good bang on the back seat?" suggests that he may indeed know about his wife's affair, which may account for his lifelong compulsion to prove his masculinity. The following exchange further reinforces his knowledge (even if on a repressed level) of Jessie's infidelty:

SAM: Yes, I leave that to others.
MAX: . . . What others? . . . Other people? What other people? (*Pause.*) What other people?

Foreshadowing his proposal to Teddy about Ruth, Max suggests that Sam bring any of his "birds" to the "house": "She can keep us all happy. We'd take it in turns to give her a walk around the park."

When the hungry son Joey appears — the athlete in training — Max's greeting hints of his own female role in the house: "Who do you think I am, your mother?" and Max calls Joey, as he has Len, "a bitch." Lenny, increasingly more infantilized, wants to ingratiate himself with his father:

You used to tuck me in bed every night. He tucked you up too, didn't he, Joey?
(*Pause.*)

The sound play on the verb is unmistakable, as the accompanying pause indicates. Joey and Max continue:

55

JOEY: He used to like tucking up his sons.
MAX: I'll give you a proper tuck up one of these nights,
son.

Max insults Joey as a "gentle/man's" boxer, calls Sam a "maggot" (again the rhyming word is suggested), and he finally recalls his own father's "dandling" him. Another blackout follows, and the teddy-bear baby Teddy and his wife, the faithful Ruth, enter. Teddy is excited to be back home, and, like a child, he runs upstairs to see if his old bed is still in his old bedroom.

Ruth, who has never met Teddy's father, immediately recognizes her husband's change in role and the potential danger of remaining in his childhood home. She suggests that they leave immediately. Teddy is caught, however, as the emasculated child, and he answers concretely: "Nothing's changed. Still the same." Self-conscious also that he is married, he is terrified of revealing his sexuality to his father:

> The only thing is we don't want to make too much noise.
> . . . There is no need to be nervous. . . . After all, we
> have to be up early, see Dad — wouldn't be quite right
> if he found us in bed, I think. (*He chuckles.*)

Ruth understandably exits for some fresh air, and Lenny enters, dressed in pajamas. Neither surprised nor pleased to see his long-lost brother, Lenny initiates their banal conversation, and after only a few minutes, Teddy goes upstairs. Ruth returns and meets Lenny, who is so threatened to learn that she is his brother's wife that he rushes on to talk in very concrete terms of a broken clock: in the nighttime, daytime problems become overwhelming. Aware of Ruth's menacing power, Lenny tries to intimidate her — he brags of his various sexual conquests and mentions a woman whose proposals he rejected because she was "diseased . . . falling apart with the pox"; so, he boasts, "I clumped her one."

Ruth recognizes his game, and her comment: "How did you

know she was diseased?" leaves Lenny more seriously threatened than before he began his tale. His absurdly honest reply, "I decided she was," occasions his rapid change of subject: how wonderful that Ted has a Ph.D. degree. But his banal chatter is punctuated with intermittent admissions of his brutality toward women.

Ruth gains more and more control, although as they toast their glasses of water she, unknowingly, assaults him by calling him "Leonard."

> LEN: Don't call me that. That's the name my mother
> gave me.

Len is at Ruth's mercy, and as he tries to remove the water, she says: "If you take the glass . . . I'll take you." The identification of Ruth, the pox-diseased woman, and the mother, has begun.

The next morning, Joey stands shadow-boxing — until his father's glance embarrasses him. Sam has cooked Max's breakfast, but apparently because of Max's not-well-repressed knowledge that his brother saw his wife's infidelity (and is therefore a witness to his own cuckoldry), he insults him. Condensing many emotional meanings in his notion of butchery, and reinforcing the equation of men and animals, Max says:

> I learned to carve a carcass at his knee [his father's]. I
> commemorated his name in blood. I gave birth to three
> grown men! All on my own bat. What have you done? You
> tit!

Teddy and Ruth finally appear among the rest of the family. No warm greetings are exchanged, Teddy is embarrassed about oversleeping, and his hesitations in introducing his wife are apparent. When Max sees Ruth, he accuses Teddy of bringing a "dirty tart," a "smelly scrubber," "a stinking pox-ridden slut" into his house. Max completes his fond name-calling as he greets Teddy: "Bitch."

57

Joey makes perhaps the first gesture of his life against his father as he excuses "an old man's" behavior. But Max takes up his stick and hits not only Joey but also Sam, who then falls to the floor. Father and son stare at each other. But Max, threatened about his potential loss of Teddy, babies him, cuddles him, laughs, and at last relaxed, says: "He still loves his father!"

Act II presents background information that well explains the father's behavior. As a young man Max had to support two families: his wife and children and, he admits resentfully, his sick mother and mentally crippled brothers. Even more revealing, Max discloses his subordinate role to his wife when their sons were children. Jessie ran the house: "She taught those boys everything they know," while he bathed them and "suffered the pains of childbirth." Max concludes his confession by calling his sons "bastards" and his wife "slut-bitch." His association of the last with Sam, who witnessed Jessie's infidelity, stirs him to even more grotesque abuses. He accuses Sam of homosexuality: "You'd bend over for half a dollar on Blackfriar's Bridge." Max brags that Mac — the nature of their friendship is never qualified — was a better driver than Sam. But Sam's response, which is not the *non sequitur* it appears, hints of that old incident: "Don't you believe it." One can well understand that, at this rate, Sam will be pushed into an admission of that primal scene.

Ruth's pose changes as Max, to her surprise, compliments her: "You're a charming woman." She replies that she was less than respectable when she first met Teddy. Max's display, it seems, has prompted her confession. To break the tension and guard against any further emotional outbursts, the two impotent intellectuals, Lenny and Teddy, begin a philosophical debate.

Much like Ionesco's pupil who can add extraordinary sums but is incapable of subtracting simple ones, Teddy cannot answer Len's question because it is "not within my province." It is Ruth who responds, by acting out the emotional meaning within their guarded language and by reaffirming the sensual basis of reality:

> LENNY: How can the unknown merit reverence? [Any speculation is only an hypothesis.]
>
> . . . .
>
> RUTH: Perhaps you misinterpret [the essentials of experience]. Action is simple. . . . My lips move. Why don't you restrict . . . your observations to that? Perhaps the fact that they move is more significant . . . than the words which come through them.

Teddy — who, in completely rationalizing his emotional life, may be the most violent character on stage — is nevertheless aware of the real exchanges of feeling before him. Realizing that he may lose the precarious stability of his ordered life with Ruth, he suddenly proposes that they return home to see their sons (like Jessie and Max, they have three), and he adds, concretely: "It's so clean there." Ruth confronts him; after all, he has forced her into this situation. She would have left this house last night. Twice, she says: "Is it dirty here?" Equating a bath with the purging of all his unpleasant thoughts, Teddy continues:

> If we can go back, we can bathe till October. . . . Here there's nowhere to bathe, except the swimming bath down the road. You know what it's like? It's like a urinal. A filthy urinal!

This comment, which reinforces Teddy's repression of self, angers Ruth, and it occasions her recollections of her past as a "model of the body." This, in turn, sexually stimulates the men in the house. Lenny and she dance; Ruth even kisses Len. Max and Joey enter, and Joey comments:

> Christ, she's wide open. Dad, look at that.
> (*Pause.*)
> She's a tart.

59

Joey then caresses Ruth, gets on top of her on the sofa, during which time Lenny fondles her hair; Joey and Ruth roll on the floor; Ruth calls out for food and drink, and the orgy is well begun.

In the last act the *status quo* is apparently resumed. Ruth asks Teddy if his family has read his books, and Teddy's reply reminds her of his sterile approach to the world, his lack of involvement, and his need to continue intellectual games whose sophistication and expertise have been unmatched since Edward's in *A Slight Ache*: "It's a question of how far you can operate *on* things, and not *in* things."

Sam enters and tries to be affectionate with Teddy (who now seems to be in Len's role of Act I). Lenny accuses Teddy of eating his cheese roll, although he praises him for his academic success. And Joey, returned from Ruth's bed upstairs, admits to Lenny that he's "not gone the whole hog," whereupon the two brag of their sexual conquests with other "birds."

When Sam and Max return and learn that Ruth is still upstairs, Max, fearful that his son may indeed realize his masculinity, screams: "Where's the whore? Still in bed? She'll make us all animals." Not only has the ex-butcher continually referred to his sons as a variety of male animals, but he has also called each "bitch." It is all right for him to wave animal sexuality before their eyes, as long as he can also emasculate them.

When Teddy (!) tells his father about Joey's unsuccessful two hours, the solicitous parent queries: "My Joey. She did that to my boy?" at which point, aware that Ruth can be an asset to him in retaining an emasculated household, he contrives a plan: They will "keep" Ruth in their house. Teddy, still incapable of expressing his feelings, offers a reasonable answer as to why she should not remain — she's not well and ought to return to her children. (We recall that Max's mother was also ill.) Max then identifies Ruth with his mother and says he is accustomed to looking after sick people.

Max's intimidation of Teddy continues: "What do you know about what she wants, eh, Ted?" Max victorious, they must next plan how to pay Ruth. She could earn a working wage from them, but better yet, the pimp Len can set her up in one of his "flats" on Greek Street. Teddy can even be the American liaison, advertising "Specials" with Ruth for visiting academicians, and perhaps he can even work out an arrangement with the airlines.

Ruth hardly hears Teddy's timid suggestion that she might still return home with him, and she busies herself with small business details involved in their new corporation. All of this is too much for Sam, who finally divulges his knowledge of Jessie and Mac and then suffers a temporary stroke.

The obvious is finally admitted, but no one much cares, except Teddy, who wants a ride to London Airport. He bids all a fond farewell, Ruth calls him Eddie and says the ironic "Don't become a stranger," and the scene is fixed as Joey places his head in Ruth's lap, which stirs Max to "move above them, backwards and forwards." The identification complete between Ruth and Jessie, Max, who fears that she finds him too old and prefers his would-be virile son Joey, says: "Listen. You think you're just going to get that big slag all the time? You think you're just going to have him . . . ?" And though he expresses his anticipation of her infidelity, "She'll do the dirty on us," he falls to his knees, crawls toward her, and pleads: "I'm not an old man. . . . Do you hear me? . . . Kiss me." Ruth continues to caress Joey's head as Max wishfully looks on.

The games here are finally divided. Teddy returns to the rituals of civilization, but his wife remains to provoke the ancient antagonisms between generations. Ironically, Eden is not innocent, nor civilization corrupt; the latter is an endless round of banal responsibilities, the former — to use Freud's phrase — "a seething cauldron" of sexual intrigues. Things are not what we suppose; but then, if they were, we would have no need for Pinter and his stratagems.

Harold Pinter was born October 10, 1930, in East London's inelegant Hackney. The only son of a Jewish tailor, he won a scholarship to a local grammar school, Hackney Downs. He pursued an early acting career by entering the Royal Academy of Dramatic Arts (1948) and joining a repertory company (1949), with which, under the stage name of David Baron, he toured throughout England and Ireland.

Pinter began writing poetry, short stories, monologues, and duologues in his teens. Once he began writing dramas in 1957, however, he abandoned all other literary projects, including his long autobiographical novel, *The Dwarfs*. That year he completed his first stage play, the one-act *The Room* and *The Dumb Waiter*, as well as the full-length *The Birthday Party*. The radio play *A Slight Ache* followed in 1959, along with several revue sketches, which marked Pinter's first popular success. His next full-length piece, *The Caretaker* (1960), brought him popularity not only in England but in America. During the five years before he completed *The Homecoming* (1965), Pinter wrote several short television and radio plays — *Night Out, Night School, The Dwarfs, The Collection, The Lover, Tea Party*, and the unfinished *The Hothouse*, his only political play. He also began his highly successful film career with an adaptation of *The Caretaker* to the screen as *The Guest*, and his scripts for *The Servant, The Pumpkin Eater*, and *Accident*. In 1967 he completed the filmscript *The Basement* for BBC television. He has subsequently embarked upon a directing career with Robert Shaw's *The Man in the Glass Booth*.

Pinter's plays have received many awards, from the New York Critics' Award to the Queen's Order of the British Empire. But his success has been hard won. During the years he began writing, his income was so precarious that he had to hold many different jobs, from caretaker, doorman, and snow-shoveler to street salesman and dance-hall bouncer. Today, with his wife, actress Vivien Merchant, and their ten-year-old son Daniel, he lives in a five-story period house in Regency Park. Pinter confesses his lifelong passions to include cricket, jazz, popular music, Berg, beer, Scotch, Picasso's and Francis Bacon's drawings, Yeats, Hardy, Philip Larkin, and Samuel Beckett.

His future plans include a film version of *The Birthday Party*. Although he has been offered several film contracts and the opportunity to work with Antonioni and Godard, he says he must return to the theater, which he finds most "exciting," "restricting," and "very naked." At the end of 1967 he was working on a play about a "woman of fifty . . . who is talking. That's all I bloody well know. I don't know who she is. Certainly it's not a room." Pinter insists that he can never again "deal with a room" and that his next play has "got to be even more naked than the last."

About the Author

LOIS G. GORDON is, at present, Assistant Professor in the Department of English at Fairleigh Dickinson University, Teaneck, New Jersey. Previously, she served as Visiting Assistant Professor at the University of Missouri–Kansas City (1966–1968) and as Lecturer in English at the City College of New York (1964–1966).

Dr. Gordon prepared for her academic career at The University of Michigan (B.A., 1960) and at The University of Wisconsin (M.A., 1962; Ph.D., 1966). In addition to several reviews of scholarly works and an article, "Pigeonholing Pinter: An Annotated Bibliography," which will be published in *Theatre Documentation,* she has written an essay on *Death of a Salesman,* which will appear in Warren French's critical volume *The Forties.* She is presently at work on a critical study of Samuel Beckett's plays. Her husband is a psychiatrist and poet.